THIS IS
WRESTLING!
TODAY'S STARS, TOMORROW'S LEGENDS

THIS IS
WRESTLING!

TODAY'S STARS, TOMORROW'S LEGENDS

George Napolitano

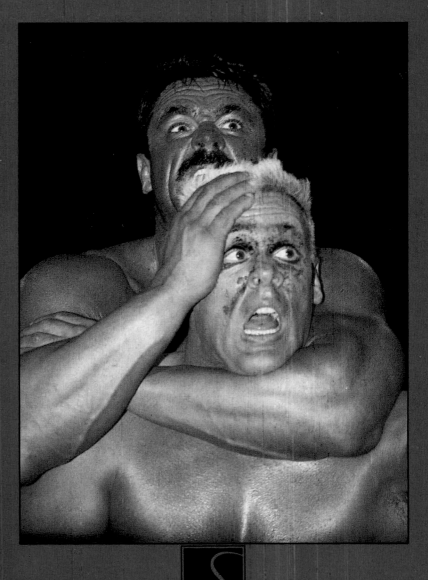

SMITHMARK

CONTENTS

This edition published in 1993
by SMITHMARK Publishers Inc.
16 East 32nd Street
New York, New York 10016.

SMITHMARK books are available for bulk purchase for sales promotion and premium use. For details write or telephone the Manager of Special Sales, SMITHMARK Publishers Inc., 16 East 32nd Street, New York, NY 10016, (212) 532-6600.

Produced by Brompton Books Corp.,
15 Sherwood Place,
Greenwich, CT 06830.

ISBN 0-8317-5165-7

Printed in China

10 9 8 7 6 5 4 3 2

Page 1: Ric Flair waves to the crowd. Considered by many to be the greatest wrestler of all time, the 6′ tall, 242-pound Nature Boy defends his many championship belts, commenting, "If anyone wants my belt, they have to walk that aisle and climb space mountain. To be the man you have to beat the man!"

Page 2: Animal throws the hefty Samoan Savage in a hard-fought match. With his size and brutal ring style, Animal often overwhelms his opponents.

Page 3: Ravishing Rick Rude has Sting in a painful hold. While Rude considers himself the sexiest man in wrestling, fan favorite Sting guarantees excitement in the ring.

Left: The 6′ 10″, 299-pound Sid Justice delivers a vicious kick to Scott Steiner, master of the devastating "Franken-steiner" move.

INTRODUCTION

As a youngster growing up in New York I used to watch wrestling on television every week. In my case it was Channel Five, and the matches were broadcast from Sunnyside Gardens in Queens, New York; the Bridgeport Arena in Bridgeport, Connecticut; and the Capital Arena in Washington, D.C.

The United States Champion was "Nature Boy" Buddy Rogers, and I dreaded every time he appeared on the screen. He was arrogant, obnoxious and – just like the New York Yankees, whom I despised with a passion – he would always win!

By hook or by crook, Rogers would invariably defeat my heroes: Cowboy Bob Ellis, Johnny Valentine, Dory Dixon, Bearcat Wright, and even the 601-pound Haystacks Calhoun. No matter who he faced, Rogers – with the help of his manager, Bobby Davis, and his figure-four leg grapevine – would always come out victorious. Every couple of months a new contender would be billed as the one who would knock off Buddy Rogers once and for all, but it never happened.

Hey, I thought I had it made when Cowboy Bob Ellis devised a way to reverse the figure-four hold.

Right then and there I told my friends, Jerry Scotti and Jerry Rallo, that their favorite was going to fall! But like the Brooklyn Dodgers, year after year, Ellis did not win. I was totally devastated. This went on month after month, year after year.

On June 30, 1961, Rogers defeated the NWA World Champion, Pat O'Conner, in Comiskey Park in Chicago in front of 38,622 people. The pompous Rogers had conquered the world!

Needless to say, I was not there, but when Rogers went on television the following week sporting his new belt and referring to himself as the new World Champion, I felt sick. Now I was going to have to hear it from my wrestling buddies. Fortunately, summer vacation came just in the nick of time, and I was not going to see the guys for two months. I figured Rogers would lose the belt by then, and then I would have something to talk about. No such luck! On the first day of school, after my nice long summer vacation, the two Jerrys were waiting to get me. Now their man was the World Champion! When he was U.S. Champ they thought he was something, but now that he was the World Champ, I did not have a leg to stand on.

For the next two years, my "good guy" wrestlers always lost to Rogers. Fortunately, I had a few favorites to cheer for who did capture Tag Team

Left: The original "Nature Boy," Buddy Rogers (right), embraces the current "Nature Boy," Ric Flair. This photo was taken shortly before Buddy's passing in 1992. Buddy wrestled in parts of five decades and was the dominant villain for almost 25 years. Ric has his own style, but there is no denying that he has been greatly influenced by Buddy.

Right: The Ultimate Warrior struts to the ring. Ultimate has had gold around his waist several times. He says that he gets his powers from "the planets." No one knows exactly what he means, but few would confront him face to face! Currently riding a wave of incredible popularity, will he stand the test of time and lead wrestling into the future? Many experts say that he could be the top star in the business for many years to come.

Left: Hulk Hogan shows the intensity of a true champion. The Hulkster has been an idol to millions of youngsters from all around the globe. He likes the limelight and uses his celebrity status to spread a positive message: "Say your prayers, stay in school, eat your vitamins and listen to your parents!" A champ in the wrestling ring, he is also a champ to the dozens of charities for which he helps raise funds. "I have been blessed by the big Hulkster in the sky – and it is the least I can do to give something back," he told me.

This is Wrestling!

Below: Randy Savage gets ready to send Ric Flair airborne! These two have battled in sold-out arenas around the world. Randy once told me that he respects Ric for his wrestling ability but finds him a bit too egotistical – an interesting analysis from the man who dubbed himself the "Macho Man!"

Right: The strongman from Abruzzi, Italy, Bruno Sammartino. The dominant "good guy" in his day, Bruno never let his fans down. A little known fact about Bruno: Before turning to wrestling, he sparred with the then boxing champion Sonny Liston and did not go down!

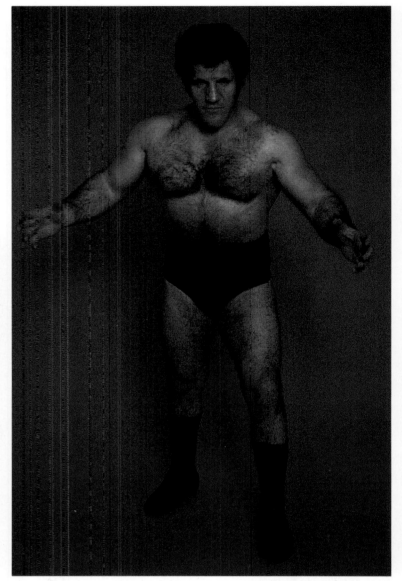

Championships, such as the Bastein Brothers, Mark Lewin and Don Curtis, and Argentina Apollo and Johnny Valentine. My friends meanwhile rooted for the "bad guy" tag teams, like the Kangaroos and the Graham Brothers.

I can not recall all the opponents who faced Rogers during his reign as World Champion, but there was one who stood out – Bruno Sammartino! He was my man, a fellow Italian, a great guy who would never break the rules. I knew from the first time I saw him on TV that he was special.

Then on May 17, 1963, Jerry Rallo called and said that his uncle would take us to the wrestling matches at Madison Square Garden that night. I was ecstatic! I was going to the fabled Madison Square Garden to see wrestling in person! I was thrilled beyond belief!

All during the preliminary matches my friend kept on needling me about how his man was going to kill my Bruno. I argued and argued with him over this, but he was persistent.

Finally it was time for the main event. There we were, way up in the upper balcony, but it did not matter! There was electricity in the air. Somehow I sensed that something was going to happen!

Left: The Steiner Brothers, Rick and Scott, have a large collection of tag team title belts. They never fail to excite the fans with their great scientific wrestling ability. "We can beat any team in the world," Scott and Rick said in unison. These two men from Michigan may be right!

Above: Sting strikes a pose. When not wrestling, the Stinger can be found in one of two places: in the gym or on the beach. "I try to work out five days a week," he said, "and I always find time to surf." This handsome champion knows how to keep his fans happy – he wins!

Far left: Look out, it's the Nasty Boys! They were bad guys for a long time, but they have also wrestled as fan favorites. Why the change? Nasty Boy Jerry Saggs told me, "Our former manager Jimmy Hart lied to us! We like being champions, and we won't need his help ever again!" Perhaps they should change their name to the "Nice Boys!"

This is Wrestling!

Right: Hulk Hogan is about to whip the massive Earthquake across the ring. The Hulkster may tip the scales as 295 pounds, but even he seems small when compared to the giant Earthquake. "He is a big dude," Hogan told me. "I think that I am the only man to body slam him, dude." Earthquake was hated by the fans for years, but after his battles against Hogan, the Quakester started to see the light. He teamed with Typhoon to form the "Natural Disasters," and while they may have broken the rules for some time, they both eventually began to cherish support from the fans. "We realized that when the fans cheer for you, it really gets your adrenalin pumped up. It became fun to see the fans rooting for us," he told me. Good or bad, the 400-pound-plus giant always impressed the fans with his physical ability. Earthquake was a Sumo champ in Japan, and it helped him with his balance when learning the American wrestling style. "I am glad that he is a good guy these days, dude," the Hulk said. "I would not want to face him again any time soon."

This is Wrestling!

When Rogers strutted into the ring, my friend went crazy. He was yelling and screaming, but everyone around us was on my side. Hearing their reaction, I really felt confident. As soon as Bruno was introduced, he ran into the ring and charged at Rogers. Bruno tossed the champ into the ropes and immediately caught him in his bear hug. Everyone around us was cheering madly. Finally Bruno dropped Rogers to the mat, and then put the exhausted Nature Boy in the Italian Back Breaker. The champ squirmed. My friend cried. Rogers signalled to the referee that he was through. He had submitted. In an instant the bell rang. After 47 seconds the ring announcer stated, "The winner and new Champion of the World, Bruno Sammartino!"

Finally, I had a winner. I was overjoyed. My friend Jerry was so upset that he did not say a word the whole ride home. The next day in school I walked around in a cloud. My friend, meanwhile, was in the dumps. Of course we had a playful fight that day because, after years and years of built-up frustration over Buddy Rogers, I had to get back at him. It was a great feeling to be on top.

After that day we had no more heated arguments over the title, but I do know my friends never got over Buddy Rogers. Years later, after I became professionally involved in the sport as a wrestling journalist, photographer and magazine editor, they would ask me whatever became of their hero. I would let them in on his whereabouts, and we would rehash old stories about our childhood wrestling fever.

For me it was Buddy Rogers versus Bruno Sammartino. For youngsters today it might be the Ultimate Warrior vs. Ric Flair, or Randy Savage vs. Razor Ramon, or Ron Simmons vs. Butch Reed, or Hulk Hogan vs. Sid Justice, or Sting vs. Jake Roberts, or Kerry Von Erich vs. the Honky Tonk Man.

Whoever are your favorites, I offer you this advice: hang in there! While life may not be perfect, in wrestling, good will eventually triumph over evil. And maybe that is the secret reason why wrestling holds such an important place in the hearts and minds of young and old alike!

George Napolitano

Left: The Barbarian and Road Warrior Hawk collide in mid-ring. These two grapplers are among the very toughest in the sport.

Far left: Yours truly with wrestling legends Andre the Giant and Bruno Sammartino at a wrestling show in 1992. This was Andre's last public appearance before his unexpected death in January, 1993.

Above left: The Mighty Hercules with two of his biggest fans, my sons Joseph and Gregory. Hercules was a guest at Gregory's last birthday party. Joseph once took Andre the Giant to school for "show and tell"!

Above: Lex Luger contemplates his next match. The 6'5" muscleman took some time off from the sport to concentrate on bodybuilding.

THE GOOD, THE BAD,

AND THE UGLY

Night after night in arenas all over the world we sit and marvel at the physiques and physical dexterity of such athletes as Hulk Hogan, Sting, Lex Luger, the Ultimate Warrior, Ron Simmons, Mr. Perfect, Rick and Scott Steiner, Razor Ramon, Tony Atlas, Tatanka, Animal, Hawk, Rick Rude and many others. Certainly it took them countless hours of training in the gym to get their bodies in such fantastic condition. But, as many people know, workouts alone won't get you a Hulk-sized physique overnight. It takes years of dedication to even get close to looking like some of your favorite wrestling stars.

Although body training for muscle tone and bulk is definitely a key to becoming a star grappler, it is only one of the requisites. A big body is just not enough to make it to the top of the wrestling game. It helps, but it takes much more.

Learning the skills of the mat – the intricate wrestling holds and maneuvers – is also required. And, even with a good wrestling background and a superbly conditioned body, there is still more needed to stand out in the wrestling business.

Far left: Hulk Hogan asks the crowd to let him hear it! "The Hulkamaniacs are more important to me than anything in the world – anything, brother!" he told me. I can verify that statement. Recently, I spent a week on the road with the big guy. He wrestled in five different cities, and he visited at least two hospitals every day to cheer up the children.

Left: Sting hoists Lex Luger on his shoulders. These two superior athletes are at the very top of their game.

Above: "Mr. Perfect," Curt Hennig, shows off his Intercontinental Belt. "This is not enough. I want the world title, and I will get the world title," promised the young grappling star. Hated by the fans for his egotistical ways, Perfect has also shown his better side at times. "I guess I should try to be more of a nice guy, but I am always focused on the challenge in front of me in the ring." Separating from Ric Flair and Bobby "The Brain" Heenan is a good first step to winning the fans over.

It is the color, the personality, the charisma of each individual athlete, or sometimes the character that they portray, that usually elevates a wrestler to the highest plateau in the game. There are no survivors in wrestling who are not versed in the fundamentals of ring technique, and it is also true that there are no survivors over any length of time who have not shown a personality – a reason to cheer for him, or a reason to boo him!

Just about every wrestler can fall into one of three categories: the Good, the Bad, and the Ugly. Good guys do not break the rules. They want to win fair and square, and the fans appreciate that. Bad guys will do whatever it takes to gain a victory, and many of them seem to relish breaking all the rules. The Ugly? Well, some bad guys are just so rotten, mentally and physically, that all I can say is that you know one when you see one!

Left, inset: **"Quien es muy macho?" asks the Cuban Razor Ramon. "I will walk all over you, Chico. Get that camera out of my face!" he scolded. Anything you say, Chico!**

Right: **Ric Flair has turned Barry Windham's world upside down. The Piledriver is such a devastating move that it has been banned in several territories! Who delivers the best piledriver? Many say that Jerry "The King" Lawler is the true master of the move. "Ric Flair stole it from me!" asserts Lawler, but Flair protests that claim: "I don't need to steal anybody's moves," said Flair. "I am the greatest wrestler to ever walk that aisle. I am the man. I am space mountain. I am the 60-minute man. I am God's gift to women. I am Slick Ric. I am the leader of the masses, and you are only a follower!" Okay, already, I get your point!**

Left: **Road Warrior Animal has that certain look in his eye. A bad attitude and 280 pounds of rippling muscle – don't cross him!**

Left: A bloodied Hulk Hogan starts his posing routine following a tough victory. "The fans demand it. They don't want Hogan to leave the ring," said Gorilla Monsoon. "They love to cheer for this man. They want to prolong the feeling and show him their undying support."

Right: The Hulkster shows off his stunning physique. What is the down side to having such a massive body? Hulk has to have all his clothing custom made. Hogan uses the same tailor as basketball star Patrick Ewing and footballer Refrigerator Perry!

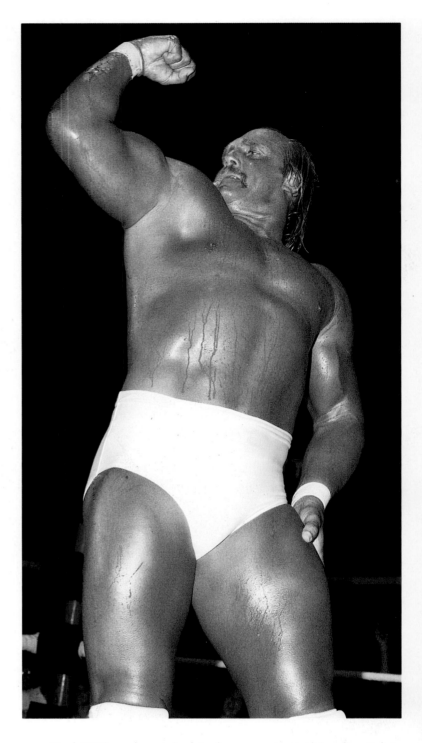

These neat categories are complicated by the fact that rather often a good guy turns bad! Tired of playing by the rules and subsequently getting taken advantage of by a bad guy, the hero can reach a boiling point and decide to take the short cut. It works the other way too – a bad guy will "see the light" and decide to play it on the up and up. His reward is the cheers of the fans!

"I got tired of listening to the referee while my opponents would do anything to hurt me," Barry Windham told me. The 6' 6" native of Sweetwater, Texas, continued, "What good are the fans when your opponent is choking you? They can't stop the pain." He may have a point, but when Windham turned bad, he broke the hearts of thousands of fans. And when he started to use vicious methods himself in the ring, well, the fans started booing him. "Let them boo, I don't need anybody," he replied. I guess we need to take Barry to a "how to win friends" seminar as soon as possible.

There are some wrestlers who most swear will never change. Hulk Hogan comes to mind. He has been a hero to millions and counts on his fans for his motivation. "Listen, brother, say your prayers, eat your vitamins and listen to the Big Hulkster in the sky," he told me. Some of today's fans may be too young to remember that Hogan was considered a bad guy early in his career and was even managed by the notorious Freddie Blassie and Luscious Johnny Valiant. But that seems long ago, and is definitely buried in the history books. Hulk follows his own personal creed and has been a role model for youngsters ever since he got hold of his first WWF World Championship belt way back in 1984. Nowadays the Hulkster divides his time between Hollywood and the WWF. The star of several action adventure movies, Hogan does have a bright future in show biz. But he will not let his Hulkamaniacs down and leave wrestling permanently.

What makes a wrestler good, bad, or ugly? Each wrestler seems to have his own reasons. It is hard to analyze every case. But I will tell you about some of the more interesting case studies that would have psychiatrists unable to get sleep, tossing and turning in their beds!

Ted DiBiase has tried to buy up everything in sight since he proclaimed himself the "Million Dollar Man." He has exhibited some of the greediest behavior ever witnessed by wrestling fans. He is a slick wheeler-dealer who is not above bribing officials to ensure a ring victory. "Listen, George, everyone has a price for the Million Dollar Man," he said. Some of his more infamous deeds? Well, he has bribed people to kiss his sweaty feet, wipe his body after a match, bark like a dog, and a variety of other tasks which seem to satisfy his sadistic streak. He has been known to pay not to wait in line, and one time he even ordered newlyweds out of their bridal suite just because he wanted the deluxe accommodations. "Don't forget to tell the fans that I am a great wrestler," he said as he slipped an envelope into my breast pocket. Don't worry, I donated the money to charity!

This is Wrestling!

Left: Second generation superstars Barry Windham and Dustin Rhodes. Barry's dad is the legendary villain Black Jack Mulligan, and Dustin's dad is the Bull of the Woods, Dusty Rhodes.

Above: The Ultimate Warrior roars in triumph. A little known fact about Warrior is that he trained with Sting, and the two of them once wrestled as a tag team during their rookie year!

Right: This rare photo of the Warrior without his face makeup was taken in Japan, where he successfully defended his world title against all comers.

The Ultimate Warrior began his career as a shadowy man of mystery. He rarely talked and was billed as being from parts unknown. At 6' 3" and 280 pounds, he was a mountain of muscle. The fans instantly liked him. One glance at him and his opponents were immediately intimidated! He is thrilling to watch in the ring. But who was this man who looked up to the moon for guidance? Not so strange, really. He says that he tries to focus on his opponent and block everything else out. So far, so good. But then he added something about getting his powers from the heavens! Whatever, this powerhouse has been the WWF World Champ, and many feel that he will be in the title picture for years to come.

Few athletes can match the strength, stamina, charisma, and box-office magnetism of Sting. His every word and his every appearance both in and out of the ring is scrutinized and documented in detail. At 6' 1" and 255 pounds of rippling muscle, Sting stands out in any crowd. The inventor of the Stinger Splash, the Venice Beach native and former WCW World Champion always pleases his fans. "I have been attacked from behind by everyone from Jake the Snake Roberts to Cactus Jack, but I always get my revenge," he said. Sting handles being called a superstar very well. "I just want to please the fans," he commented.

This is Wrestling!

In the interest of inflating his already immense ego as wrestling's leading ladies man, Ravishing Rick Rude has been running afoul of almost anyone in the sport who displays even the least shred of decency. In addition, with his prancing and cavorting about inside the ring, and kissing women until they faint on the mat, the Ravishing One has shown how irresistible he is to women everywhere. He also is attracted to championship belts. He has held the WWF Intercontinental Belt and the WCW U.S. Belt, in addition to others. He also changes managers almost as often as he changes his women. His last few managers were Bobby Heenan, Paul E. Dangerously and Madusa. "I only wrestle for the money," he told me, "the women would come to me even if I wasn't a wrestler." Quick, get this man a humility pill!

Randy Savage is another wrestler who considers himself macho. In fact, that is what he is most often referred to as: "the Macho Man." Savage has been both fan favorite and villain. What motivates him? No one knows for sure. "I have beaten him up pretty bad on many occasions," said Razor Ramon. But Savage got his revenge, and injured the big Cuban, almost putting him out of wrestling forever!

Left: Paul E. Dangerously in happier times with his two top wrestlers, Ravishing Rick Rude and Stunning Steve Austin. Rude considers himself the sexiest man in wrestling. Austin just claims to be "stunning"! Dangerously makes no such claims, but people say that he uses his always-present portable phone to constantly call those romance hot-lines!

Right: The Undertaker stalks the ring. He is part human, part vampire. His dreaded Tombstone maneuver has permanently injured many of his foes. "Don't get in the ring with my man," warned manager Paul Bearer, "unless you want to meet your maker." Undertaker told me that he has seen his favorite movie, *Night of the Living Dead,* over 100 times. Contrary to what people might think, Undertaker is a real cut-up in the locker room. I have seen him do his famous Dracula impression to amuse the crew.

Left: The Macho Man Randy Savage spreads his wings like a proud peacock. "Oh yeaaah, nobody has the style of the Macho Man," he said. Randy told Arsenio Hall that he has over 200 of these outrageous outfits.

The sinister presence of the Undertaker walking into the ring is enough to scare most people attending the matches – but when he begins to dissect his opponents piece by piece in his slow, methodical manner, he sends chills of fear up the backs of fellow wrestlers. They dread stepping into the ring with the big red-headed ghoul. His expressionless face, dark-circled eyes and pale complexion have made more than one opponent stand motionless before him prior to being beaten into oblivion and mercifully finished off with the tombstone piledriver. His manager, Paul Bearer, is the only one who seems to control him, and even Ric Flair has had trouble gaining a pinfall victory over him. "He is just too awesome," said Paul Bearer as he clutched the urn that he always carries with him, heading off into his own personal darkness.

Above left: Paul Bearer clutches his prized urn. How would you like this man as your neighbor? Paul said, "I don't bother anybody. Really. Why should people complain about the hearse parked in my driveway? What business is it of theirs if I have tombstones on my front lawn? I just want to be left alone." This guy makes Gomez Adams look normal!

Above: Ric Flair looks into the face of death! "I fear no man," Flair told me after this match. "But this

guy feels no pain. I am not sure if he is human!"

"The Undertaker is not human," explained his manager Paul Bearer. "He is from the dark side!"

Right: Ron Simmons shows off his winning physique. As the WCW World Champion, Simmons turned back the challenges of the Barbarian, Cactus Jack, and Big Van Vader. Ron spends a lot of time working with youth groups. "It's important for me to try and help," he said.

This is Wrestling!

Ron Simmons is one wrestler who has seen the light. A former football star, Simmons worked hard at becoming a great wrestler, and did make it to the top when he defeated Big Van Vader to capture the WCW World Title. Early in his career he was under the influence of the evil "Woman," who convinced him and his then partner Butch Reed to break the rules. Simmons changed for the better and never fails his fans. "I feel a responsibility to be good to my fans. They mean everything to me, and I will not let them down."

Nailz is the 6' 10" ex-convict who has done hard time in the slammer. "I don't consider him an ex-con," said the Big Bossman, "he is a con and will always be one!" Bossman should know. He has had a running feud with Nailz ever since the time that the convict stole his nightstick and used it on him to send him to the hospital. "I will never forget that," Bossman told me. "Law and order will prevail," he added.

The Honky Tonk Man lives in Honkyland, U.S.A., and drives a 1959 pink Cadillac. Where is Honkyland? It is a five house compound right outside of Memphis, Tennessee, fit for a king. "I am the king of rock and roll," Honky told me. "I shake, rattle and roll all over my opponents." That's true if your name is Ricky Steamboat, Bret Hart or Randy Savage. Honky held the WWF Intercontinental Belt longer than any other man. "That was one of my L.P. records – long playing," he laughed as he adjusted his $25,000 diamond encrusted jumpsuit. Honky sang one of his hit songs on the Arsenio Hall TV show, and almost hit his host over the head with his guitar. That's what I call a guest shot!

Left: The former WCW World Champion Big Van Vader with his manager Harley Race. These two characters will do anything to win, including using this metal shoulder adornment as a weapon!

Right, above: Nailz the Convict has the temporary advantage over the Lawman, Big Bossman. Bossman was beaten by his own nightstick on this night, but Nailz has suffered the consequences time and time again in rematches around the world.

Right, below: "Elvis? Elvis who?" says the Honky Tonk Man. "I am the greatest singer of all time. I am also the greatest Intercontinental Champ of all time," he added. He has a point, having held the IC Belt longer than any other wrestler in history. Both Randy Savage and Greg Valentine have had Honky break his guitar over their heads! "Those were some of my greatest hits," Honky explained.

Ric Flair is called the Nature Boy by friend and foe alike. He has walked that aisle as a villain and as a fan favorite. He has done it all in wrestling – he has been World Champ many times, and has been the top attraction in both the WCW and the WWF. His battles against the Ultimate Warrior for the world title have energized fans around the globe. "I am the 60-minute man," he said. "To be the man, you have to beat the man! Woooooooh." Flair is in fact the "man," but Mr. Perfect has much to say about that. "Ric Flair knows how to style and profile, but only I am perfect!" said Flair's former advisor and manager.

Left: Ric Flair, wearing one of his $25,000 robes, with 10 pounds of gold around his waist. Ric once gave me personal flying lessons in his private plane. Other wrestlers who have their pilot's license are Larry Zbyszko and Rugged Ronnie Garvin.

Above: Ric Flair applies the feared figure-four leg lock on the Macho Man Randy Savage. Referee Earl Hebner is looking at Savage, waiting for him to submit. But Savage fought his way to the ropes and the hold was broken.

Right: Flying Brian Pillman says that he is number one among the light heavyweights in the business. Most think that he is correct!

Pound for pound, Flying Brian Pillman is probably one of the best wrestlers anywhere. He specializes in taking on competitors who not only outweigh him, but sometimes also tower over him. Pillman goes into these encounters with tremendous odds against him. He emerges with more than his share of wins, impressing fans in the process and sending a message to other wrestlers not to mess with the former Cincinnati Bengals star.

Other wrestlers who have played pro football include Steve Williams, Paul Orndorff, Black Jack Mulligan, Indian Chief Wahoo McDaniel, Dangerous Danny Spivey and Lex Luger. These men are not to be played with. Williams is recognized as one of the strongest men in the sport, and one can see his awesome strength demonstrated when he delivers his patented Oklahoma Stampede move.

Above: **Brian Pillman caught in the act! Japanese superstar Jushin Liger never quite recovered from this crushing blow to his back. "I will do whatever it takes to win," Pillman said. "I used to follow the rules, but rules are for suckers!" What a winning attitude from this young man!**

Right: **The "Total Package" Lex Luger shows off his physique. Lex was injured in a motorcycle accident which kept him out of action for over a year, but few doubt that Luger can capture world titles if he makes that his goal. "I am the future of wrestling," he boasted. "I have conquered all who have stood before me, and I will conquer any who challenge me in the future!"**

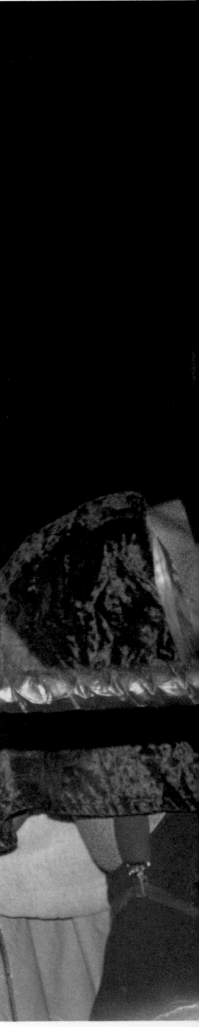

Lex Luger is a former World Champion who displays the discipline necessary to stay on top. The "Total Package" took almost a year off from the business to concentrate on bodybuilding, but now he has returned to the mat wars, and many predict that he could be the dominant wrestler for years to come.

Papa Shango and Kimala should be the best of friends. Each believes in voodoo, and each comes from Africa. But apparently, they are quite different. Shango uses his mystical powers to cause his opponents great pain by hexing them even before the match begins. He once set the Ultimate Warrior's boots on fire! Kimala chooses to use his awesome 380 pounds to splash his opponents and thereby win his matches. Shango travels with Dr. Harvey Whippleman, who somehow gets him from town to town, and Kimala is assisted by Kimchee — the only man who can control the Ugandan Giant. Shango eats raw snakes for a snack, and Kimala opts for human flesh! Better stay away from these two around dinner time!

Dustin Rhodes is called "the Natural" because he certainly possesses all the tools necessary to be a top star. The son of the legendary Dusty Rhodes, Dustin stands 6' 6" tall and has mastered the bulldog move that usually leads to victory. He explained, "Wrestling is in my blood, and I have to make my daddy proud." By winning match after match, he surely has.

Above: **The evil voodoo man Papa Shango has Hulk Hogan caught in the ropes and shows no mercy as he attempts to choke the life out of the Hulkster. "Who doo, voodoo, and conjuring," Shango told me, "Emma was a witch, Heidi was a witch, Brooha, Brooha," he rambled on meaninglessly. I think he needs a media advisor before he gives his next interview.**

Right: **The Haitian voodoo man with his smoking skull. Bobby Heenan told me that Shango was a top witchdoctor before entering the wrestling business. "He didn't make house calls, though!"**

Left: Kimala the Ugandan Giant does not like having his picture taken. This cannibal is not exactly a people person, except around dinner time. That's when he does like people – well-done, please!

Right: "The Natural" Dustin Rhodes sends Stunning Steve Austin up and over. "I just try to wrestle by the rules, and make my daddy proud of me," explained the fan favorite Dustin. The loudmouth Austin objected: "What trash! I will teach him a lesson if I can ever get a rematch!" Keep dreaming, Steve!

Right: Scott Steiner seems to have the situation under control! The future looks bright for the younger of the two Steiner Brothers. With his brother Rick they have captured several tag team belts, and on his own he won the WCW TV Title. "I prefer to wrestle with my brother, but sometimes it is good to go out solo and see what you can do," he explained.

Left: **Scott Steiner has his opponent caught in the "Frankensteiner" move. One second later Scott will be right side up and his foe will be in pain. "Scott has so much raw talent that it is scary," Theodore R. Long told me.**

Above: **Arn "the Enforcer" Anderson tries to toss a bloody Rick Steiner to the canvas. This gruelling match ended in a draw. "I give him credit," Anderson admitted, "Rick is one determined guy."**

Rick and Scott Steiner keep wrestling all in the family. These two brothers are sensational, whether as a tag team or in solo matches. Scott has perfected a move called the "Frankensteiner," which flips his opponent upside down and leads to a pinfall. Rick delivers a flying elbow off the top rope that few have gotten up from. As a team they have been World Champs, and one can only wonder if any team will be able to beat them!

This is Wrestling!

Davey Boy Smith is a former Intercontinental Champ, and so is his brother-in-law, Bret Hart. In fact, Davey Boy won the title by beating Bret in a scientific match at a packed Wembley Stadium in England at Summer Slam. Their family ties have certainly been put to the test, and they have survived.

The Bushwhackers are cousins from New Zealand who now live in America. Butch and Luke are loved by the fans, and they have been known to smash kiwi fruit into the eyes of their foes. Their wrestling tactics usually consist of illegal double-teaming and various other nefarious moves, but still the fans adore them. It must be their great smiles and winning personalities!

Above: Bret "the Hitman" Hart captured the coveted WWF World Title, thrilling his legions of fans. "It was always my number one goal and I owe it to all my fans," said the humble Hart.

Above right: The British Bulldog Davey Boy Smith has risen to the top of the wrestling game, and many predict that the world title may soon be his!

Right: Those wacky Bushwhackers send Kevin Sullivan for a ride while Kimala is cornered!

Far right: Butch shows off the secret to the Bushwhackers' success: using Luke's head as a battering ram!

Pages 42-43: Cactus Jack and Hot Stuff Eddie Gilbert during a vicious barbed wire match.

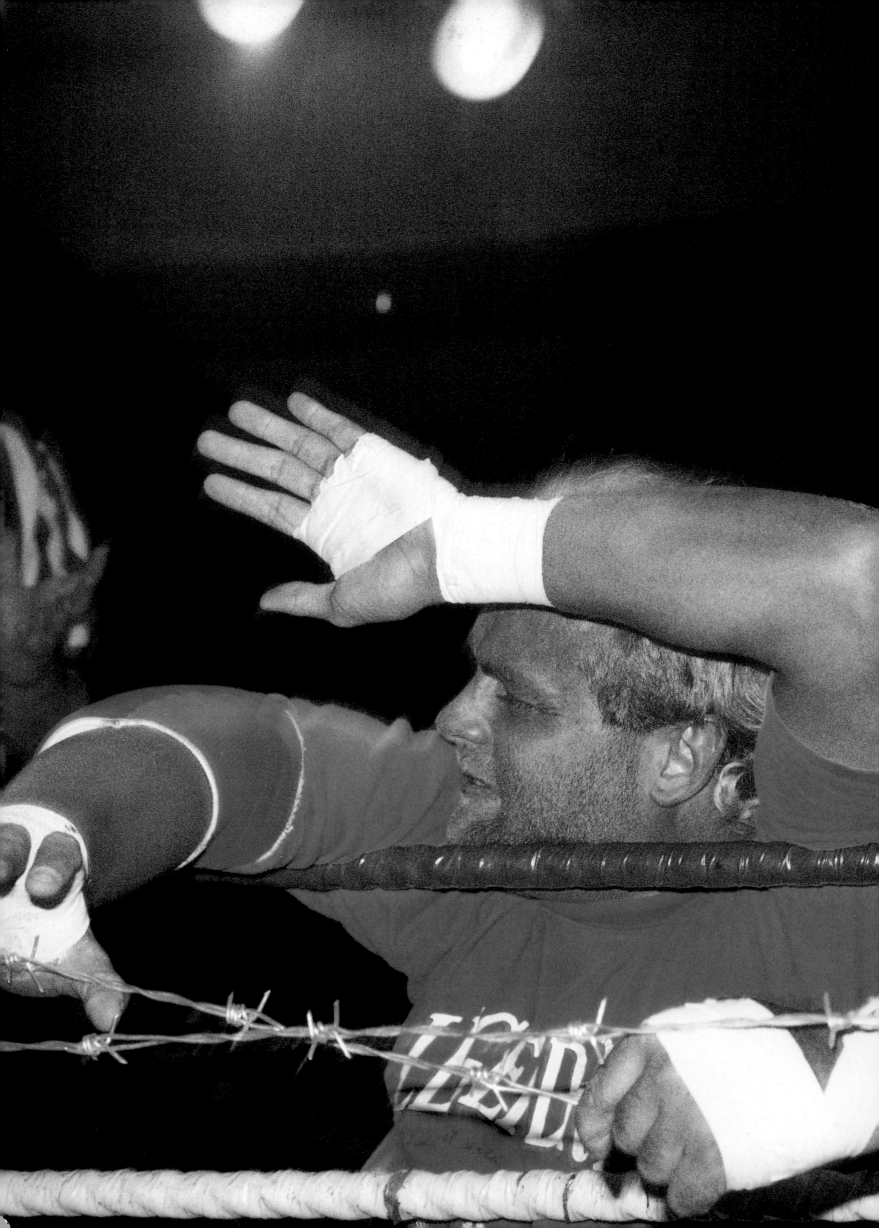

This is Wrestling!

Left: Cactus Jack and Abdullah the Butcher don't need a ring and a referee to have a fight! These two battled backstage in an arena that was going to set up for a rodeo the following night!

Right: Johnny B. Badd poses prettily for the camera. This man could appear on "Love Connection" and win a date with himself!

Below: Cactus Jack has Johnny B. Badd in a front face-lock. Though it was painful, Badd was more concerned that his hair was getting messed up!

Cactus Jack has a personality that must make even his mother cower. "I will do anything anytime anywhere to win," said Cactus between bites of his raw meat sandwich. "I do not care if I have to break a rib, an ankle or a back — I will make my opponent suffer," explained the bad man from Truth or Consequences, New Mexico. Thanks for clearing that up.

Stunning Steve Austin is also known to have a somewhat less than engaging personality. "I am stunning. I am the best looking and also the best wrestler ever," bragged the 6' 3" Texan.

Challenging Austin on his claim of good looks is Johnny B. Badd. "I am a bad man, but also a pretty man," Johnny told me. The Little Richard look-alike from Macon, Georgia, has battled Austin dozens of times with no clear-cut winner. "I have beaten him in the ring and I can also beat him in front of any mirror," Badd said.

Arn Anderson is one wrestler who cannot stand for such nonsensical talk. Known as the Enforcer, Arn settles his feuds by inflicting pain on his hapless opponents. "I am a wrestler. It is what I do best. I like to win, so therefore I win," said the Enforcer.

The Boston Bad Boy also has much to say about himself. "I am a master of strategy. I know exactly how to defeat my opponent," said the 6' 6", 280-pound former bouncer from Boston's Red Light District. "In the combat zone you learn quick that it is kill or be killed, and I have learned that well." BBB also handles a stable of evil wrestlers, and with his influence on them you can be sure that there will be a lot of pain inflicted when they are around!

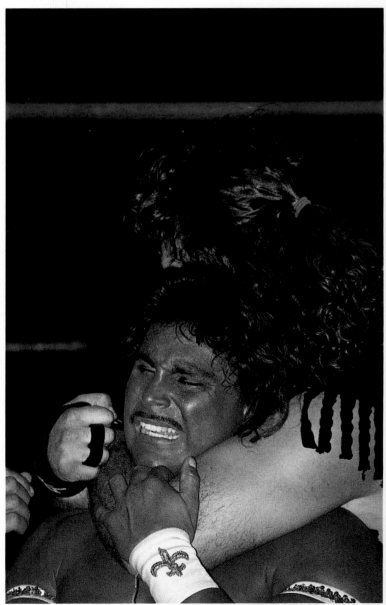

Above: Look, up in the air, it's a bird, it's a plane, it's . . . it's Superfly Jimmy Snuka caught in mid-air, about to land on Tony Atlas!

Left: Here's the Boston Bad Boy Tony Rumble with his latest discovery, the Tazmaniac! "He is part man, part beast," Rumble told me. "He is not the kind of person you would ever invite over to your house to play cards, or whatever. He is evil, he is dastardly, and he is just plain mean!" Aside from that he's a nice guy!

Right: Arn Anderson limbers up before a match backstage. Anderson is considered one of the elite group of wrestlers who is scientifically skilled in technique, and also able to brawl with the best of them.

Pages 48-49: Road Warrior Hawk delivers an awesome drop kick to Mike Rotundo. Hawk has a simple philosophy on life: "I like to beat people up!" he said. I guess Hawk will not need to rent a tuxedo and fly to Stockholm to accept the Nobel Peace Prize anytime soon!

This is Wrestling!

The original Legion of Doom or Road Warriors, Hawk and Animal make up the most awesome tag team in wrestling history. They captured the world title in whatever league they were in, and were considered indestructible. Each of them possesses superior stamina, muscle tone and wrestling knowledge. Whether wrestling as a team, or individually, these two men are feared by everyone. Hawk truly enjoys hurting people. "What a rush!" is how he described it to me. Animal has also been known to crack a few bones. Just ask the Beverly Brothers, who barely survived a confrontation with him!

Tatanka is an American Indian who loves hearing the cheers of the crowd. Dressed in his full tribal gear, he always makes a smashing entrance. He also usually smashes his opponents. In his battles against Ric "the Model" Martel, Tatanka displayed his growing wrestling skills and was able to humiliate the egotistical Martel. Tatanka is considered one of the bright future stars in all of wrestling. "I will not let him get to the top," commented Martel. "I will eventually get him so bad that he will have to retire," said the arrogant Martel.

Shawn Michaels is another grappler who has more than a trace of arrogance. Managed by Sensational Sherri, Michaels never leaves home without his trusty mirror. "Mirror, mirror on the wall, who is the toughest wrestler of them all?" he asks himself. Sherri better not hold that mirror the wrong way, she could crack it!

Left: Road Warrior Hawk will come crashing down sometime soon! His opponent Steve Williams may have evaded this blow, but he did not survive the match. Hawk is one of the few wrestlers who has captured titles in every major promotion!

Right: Sting was catapulted off the top rope and was caught by Road Warrior Animal. Sting spends a lot of time flying through the air. His Stinger Splash maneuver has left many an opponent helpless! When Sting is in the ring there should be an air traffic controller nearby!

This is Wresting!

Sid Justice is a wrestler who does not know what he sees when he looks in a mirror. Sometimes he is a good guy, and a friend to Hulk Hogan. But sometimes, he calls himself Sid Vicious and is a fierce rulebreaker. What comes over him? No one knows for sure, and nobody can ever really trust the 6' 10", 299-pound monster!

Speaking of trust, when was the last time that Jake the Snake Roberts won any friends? The evil Snakeman has attacked everyone from Sting to Dustin Rhodes. ''I am evil. I have seen the dark side. I walk alone,'' said Roberts. Wow, with an attitude like that it is no wonder that people fear this man, not to mention the 12-foot boa constrictor in his bag!

One man not afraid of Roberts is Ricky Steamboat. He and the Snakeman have grappled many times throughout the years. ''He seems to follow me wherever I go, and it's okay with me. I will not let him spook me with his giant snake,'' said the brave Steamboat. Ricky knows something about animals himself, earning the nickname, ''The Dragon.''

Above: Sid Justice plays up to the crowd! This giant of a man has never backed down from a challenge, but he needs to be watched because many think that he may be secretly jealous of Hulk Hogan and could turn bad at any moment!

Left: Ricky ''the Dragon'' Steamboat with his favorite pet, named Vince! The Dragon is well versed in wrestling skills and usually does not need to bring any intimidating serpents to the ring with him to gain the advantage.

Right: The Great Muta is one of the most mysterious men in wrestling. He possesses great skills and has tremendous stamina, yet he often resorts to cheating! Speaking through an interpreter, Joji Inoue, he said, ''Get that camera out of here. Leave me alone!''

This is Wrestling!

Koko B. Ware is a wrestler friendly with animals. In fact, he travels with his pet cockatoo, Frankie. Teaming with Owen Hart, they make an exciting and high-flying tag team. "They travel through the air so much they should make a fortune in frequent flier miles," said wrestling authority Black Jack Brown.

Another wrestler who made his mark in the sport with his high-flying moves was Kerry Von Erich, whose tragic death early in 1993 shocked the wrestling world. Known during his career as the Texas Tornado, Von Erich won titles in both the WWF and NWA, and specialized in downing his opponents with drop kicks followed by his patented tornado punch.

A notorious villain, Kevin Sullivan does not deliver any drop kicks to his opponents. "Why should I?" he asked me. "I would rather stick my finger in their eyes and hear them yell out in agony!" he explained. Kevin and his sometimes partner in crime, the evil "Woman," have wreaked havoc in every territory that they have been in. "I am assembling a group of fellow evildoers right now who will be the meanest, nastiest and most vicious men ever to enter the ring. We have many targets, and one of them might be the Ultimate Warrior!" he warned.

The good, the bad and the ugly. I leave it to you to decide just who is who!

Left: **Owen "The Rocket" Hart with his talking bird, Pat. Lately he has been teaming with another bird lover, Koko B. Ware. Together they have defeated the Beverly Brothers and have their sights set on the world tag team title. Owen comes from good wrestling stock. His father was the famous Stu Hart, and his brother is former WWF Champ Bret Hart!**

Right: **The devilish Kevin Sullivan with his valet, the fallen angel, Woman! What drives this sinister couple to cause mayhem wherever they go? "I don't know, its just the fate of the third eye – the forbidden tree from the darkened jungle – the will of Angel Heart," he ranted. Don't ask me to explain that – just be sure to avoid this pair at all costs!**

AWAY FROM THE RING

Most wrestlers lead very private lives. Their schedule of continually traveling from city to city makes family life difficult indeed. Add the pressures of keeping in shape, handling business affairs and the constant aches, pains and injuries that all professional wrestlers suffer from, and you have a formula for failure for the average man. But wrestlers are not average. They are exceptional. They are athletes as well as showmen. They participate in a sport and also a form of entertainment. It takes a superior individual to have all the skills necessary to be a successful wrestler.

Some of the top stars spend all their free time in the gym. Some, like Ricky Steamboat, make time to be with their families whenever possible. Some are cowboys who have invested their money in the land. Stan Hansen owns a large spread in Mississippi, and Black Bart has 600 acres in Texas.

Above: Film stars Tracy Ullman and Matthew Broderick are flanked by the wrestling tag team "Double Trouble" and manager Tony Rumble, "the Boston Bad Boy," at John's in New York City.

Left: Road Warrior Hawk pumps up! "Dedication, brother, that's what it takes," he explained. "After a good workout I feel like going out and crushing some bones!"

Right: Mr. and Mrs. Ron Simmons enjoy a night out on the town. The happy couple have been known to frequent the opera and the ballet. And you thought that Rugged Ron only knew about inflicting pain!

This is Wrestling!

Playboy Buddy Rose has the world's largest collection of wrestling videotapes, and James E. Cronette is not far behind.

Female grapplers Magnificent Mimi, Trudy Adams and Misty Blue have all appeared in movies, with varying degrees of success.

Jesse "the Body" Ventura, King Kong Bundy, the Haiti Kid, Andre the Giant, Big John Studd, and Rowdy Roddy Piper have also lit up the silver screen.

The giant 7' 10" El Gigante plays basketball (what else?) and Tim Horner, Robert Gibson and Ricky Morton are avid softball players. Ricky Morton of the Rock & Roll Express could also be considered a pool hustler. "It is something I have been playing since I was a teenager. My father bought me my first stick," he explained. One night Morton and his adversary Tommy Rich couldn't settle their differences in the ring, but did during an all-night session at the pool hall. Morton won 11 games to 9!

Nikolai Volkoff practices magic tricks on unsuspecting fans and Sexy Sunny Beach is a master with his surfboard.

Mr. Perfect has a career as a pro golfer if he ever wants to leave wrestling, and so does Tony Atlas.

Left: Trudy Adams, the lovely farmer's daughter, has thrilled wrestling fans with her moves in the ring. As a model and actress, she has also thrilled rock 'n' roll fans with her moves in many an MTV rock video!

Right: Hulk Hogan as he appeared in New Line Cinema's feature film, *Suburban Commando.* "I dig being an actor in the movies, but nothing replaces the rush I get when I see a little Hulkster cheering for me during a match," Hogan explained. "Hopefully I will continue to act in the movies, and also spend time in the ring. I want to do both!" Mike Fleming, of the influential entertainment trade magazine, *Variety,* said, "Hogan is a true star. He is being marketed as a movie superhero and his merchandising potential continues to grow!" No matter how you say it, Hulk Hogan is the greatest star ever to emerge from the wrestling scene.

Left: Jesse "the Body" Ventura as he appeared in the film, *Running Man.* Jesse is not just a famous actor and grappler. Did you know that he is also the mayor of his hometown, Brooklyn Park, Minnesota? How does he find the time to wrestle, act in movies and govern? "You would be surprised just how similar all three of these jobs really are," he commented. He said it, not I!

Left: **Rowdy Roddy Piper on the set of his movie,** *They Live.* **"I was made for the movies," the Scottish wrestler told me.**

Above: **Slick Ric Flair participates as a celebrity chef during a charity function.**

Above right: **Nikita Koloff toured Washington, D. C., shortly after becoming an American citizen.**

And some wrestlers are just plain old party animals. Ric Flair comes to mind. He celebrates his ring victories by taking his friends out and buying the champagne. When people call Ric Flair a "party animal," they know what they are saying. "Oh sure, I train during the day – but the nighttimes are mine!" said Flair. "I spend hours on the stairmaster because it makes me a better wrestler, and also because it makes me a better lover, whoooo!" Ric explained. Hawk is another party guy. So is Razor Ramon.

Razor Ramon may be awfully mean in the ring, but he loves to be the center of attention when he goes partying. At "Rascals," an "in spot" for wrestlers to go to when they appear in the New York area, Ramon is a legend. One night he made a splash by giving out $100 bills as tips to the deejay, waitresses, bartenders and even the men's room attendant. "I am the best at wrestling, and I am the best at night-clubbing," said Ramon. "I am always the last one left standing on the dance floor!" he boasted.

Jim "The Anvil" Neidhart usually wins his matches, and he also usually wins strongman competitions at various clubs and fairs. "I have to enter under an assumed name, and wear a disguise," the powerhouse told me.

Greg "The Hammer" Valentine spends a lot of time in local pubs. But not to imbibe – he enjoys throwing darts. "It relaxes me," said Greg. When people look at the massive wrestler, few believe that he could have the precise skill needed to throw darts. "I have won more money at the dart board than your average pool hustler," he told me.

This is Wrestling!

Left: Madusa is more than just a great wrestler and a superb manager. She is also an accomplished singer. She is currently working on an album of original tunes. Michael P.S. Hayes is lending his ear for the project.

Right: The Honky Tonk Man goes shopping for a new guitar. Known for using his guitar as a weapon, Honky has broken hundreds of them over his hapless opponents' heads. The Memphis Legend seems to like this electric baby and may use it on his next hit album, or maybe the next good guy wrestler he faces in the ring!

Far right, above: Terry Taylor sits atop one of his dozen motorcycles. "I like to ride. What are you going to do about it?" challenged Terrible Terrence. Lighten up, Terry!

Far right, below: Manager Jimmy Hart poses next to one of the vintage cars in his private collection. This 1955 Bel Air Convertible is just one of the dozen or so he owns. He should thank the Honky Tonk Man, who catapulted Hart into stardom and financial success when he allowed the "Colonel" to manage him.

Right: Do you recognize Road Warrior Animal without his face paint? The strongman has six sportscars in his garage!

The men who make up the sport of wrestling are diverse. They each give something to the public, and the public gives them something back. Love them, hate them, admire them, whatever, the professional wrestler of today is part athlete and part entertainer. Go see the matches live, and you will have a great time. No other sport offers this special kind of excitement, and no other form of sports entertainment comes even close to evoking the full range of human emotions that you will experience while watching. See you at the matches!

INDEX

ACKNOWLEDGMENTS

This book would not have been possible if it were not for the help of many
people. First and foremost, a big hug for my wife, Jacqueline, and my two
sons, Gregory and Joseph. I would also like to thank the following people
for their help and support with this project: Steve Ciacciarelli, Gary Juster,
Ray Dariano, Mike Allen, Blackjack Brown, The Slammer, Scott Record, John
and Roberta Bohan, Bob and Marci, Michael Bensen, Koichi Yoshizawa,
Robert D'Onfrio, Michael Fleming, Max Sabrin, Sal Ivone, Freddie Colon, Joji
Inoue, Jean Martin, Tony of the Press Box Cafe, Blue Stephanos of Rascals,
Mitch the Pitch, Barbara Thrasher (my favorite editor), and my agent,
Lonnie Hanover of Hanover Communications in New York.

   The publisher would also like to thank Adrian Hodgkins, who designed
the book, Jennifer Cross, who indexed it, and Cliff Lipson/New Line Camera,
who provided the copyrighted photograph on page 59.